I0815513

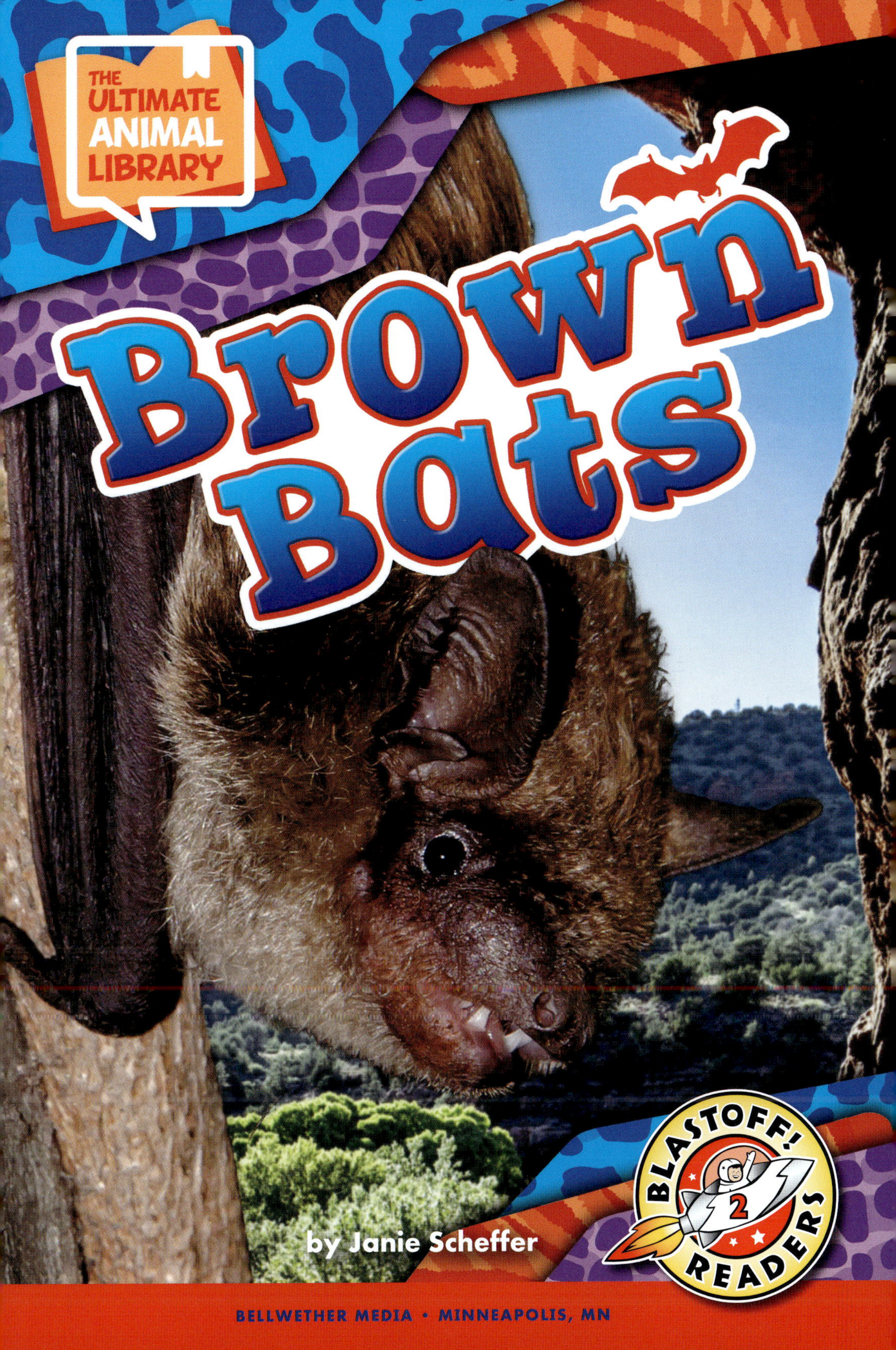
THE ULTIMATE ANIMAL LIBRARY
Brown Bats
by Janie Scheffer
BLASTOFF! 2 READERS
BELLWETHER MEDIA • MINNEAPOLIS, MN

Blastoff! Readers are carefully developed by literacy experts to build reading stamina and move students toward fluency by combining standards-based content with developmentally appropriate text.

Level 1 provides the most support through repetition of high-frequency words, light text, predictable sentence patterns, and strong visual support.

Level 2 offers early readers a bit more challenge through varied sentences, increased text load, and text-supportive special features.

Level 3 advances early-fluent readers toward fluency through increased text load, less reliance on photos, advancing concepts, longer sentences, and more complex special features.

★ **Blastoff! Universe**

Reading Level

This edition first published in 2026 by Bellwether Media, Inc.

Library of Congress Cataloging-in-Publication Data

LC record for Brown Bats available at: https://lccn.loc.gov/2025003944

Editor: Elizabeth Neuenfeldt   Series Designer: Veah Demmin

Printed in the United States of America, North Mankato, MN.

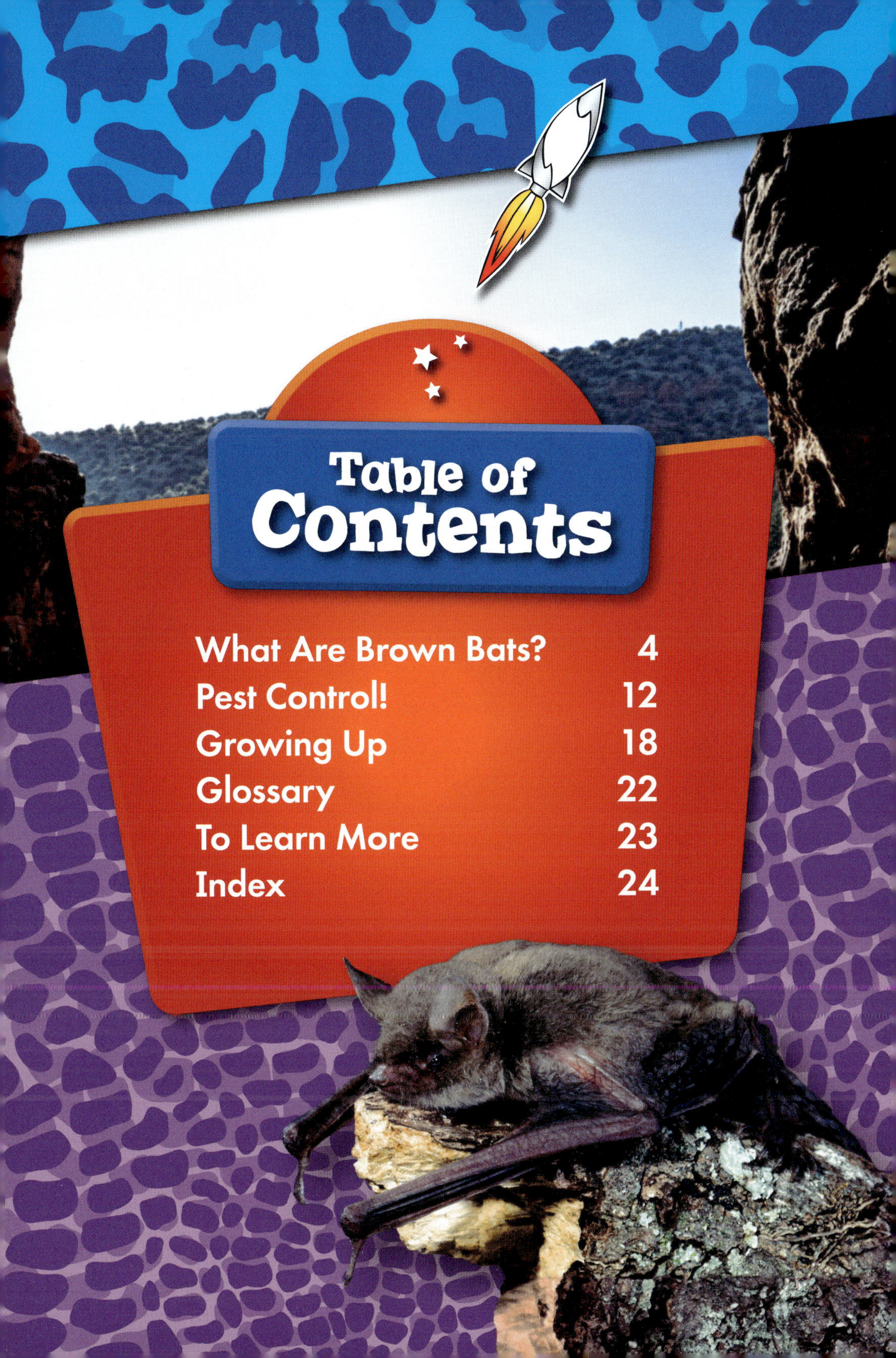

Table of Contents

What Are Brown Bats?

Brown bats are flying **mammals**.
There are big and little brown bats.
They mostly live in North America.
These helpful animals eat pests!

Little Brown Bat Report

Range

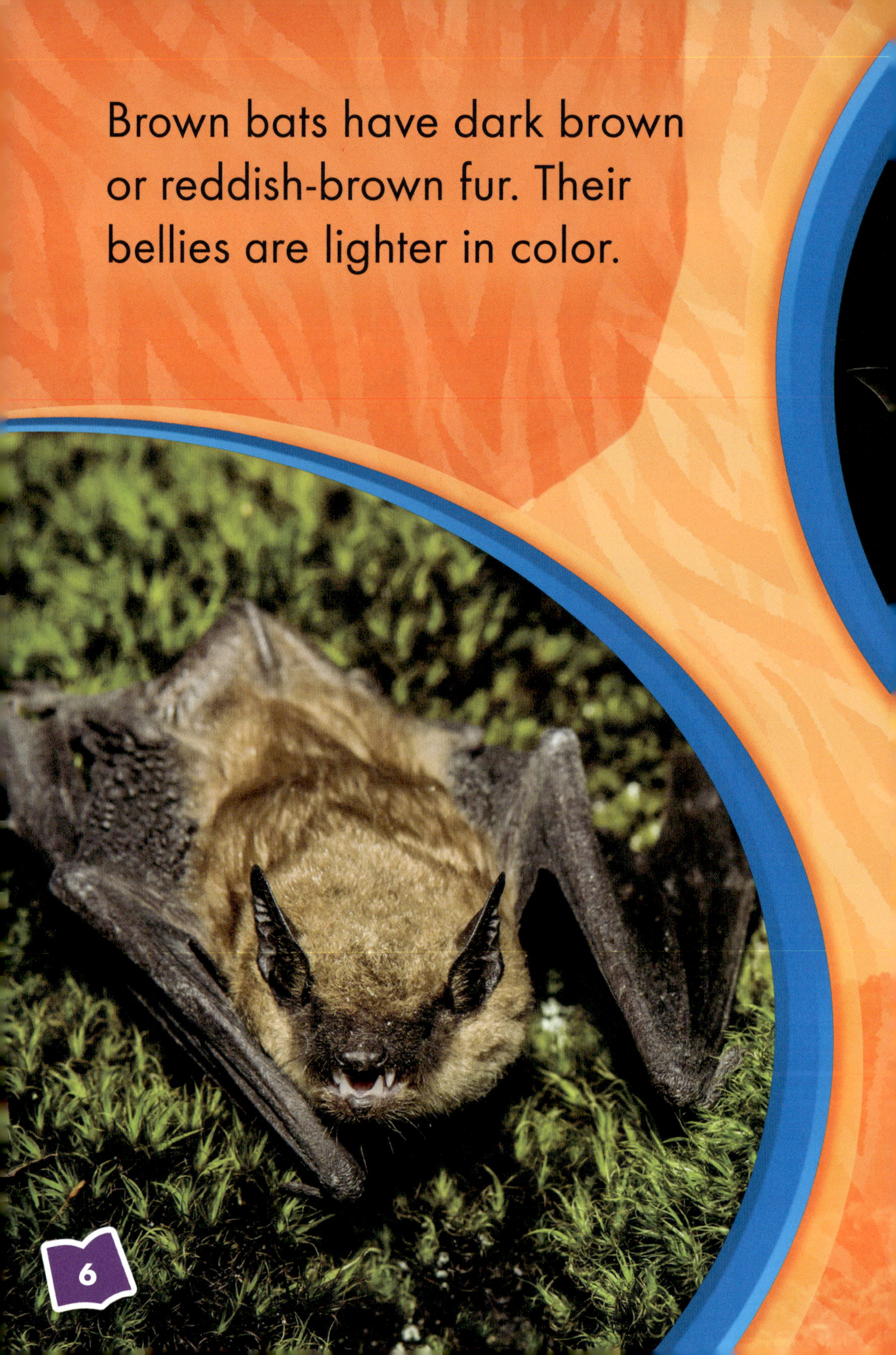

Brown bats have dark brown or reddish-brown fur. Their bellies are lighter in color.

Their wings are dark brown or black.

Brown bats have **flexible** wings made of skin.

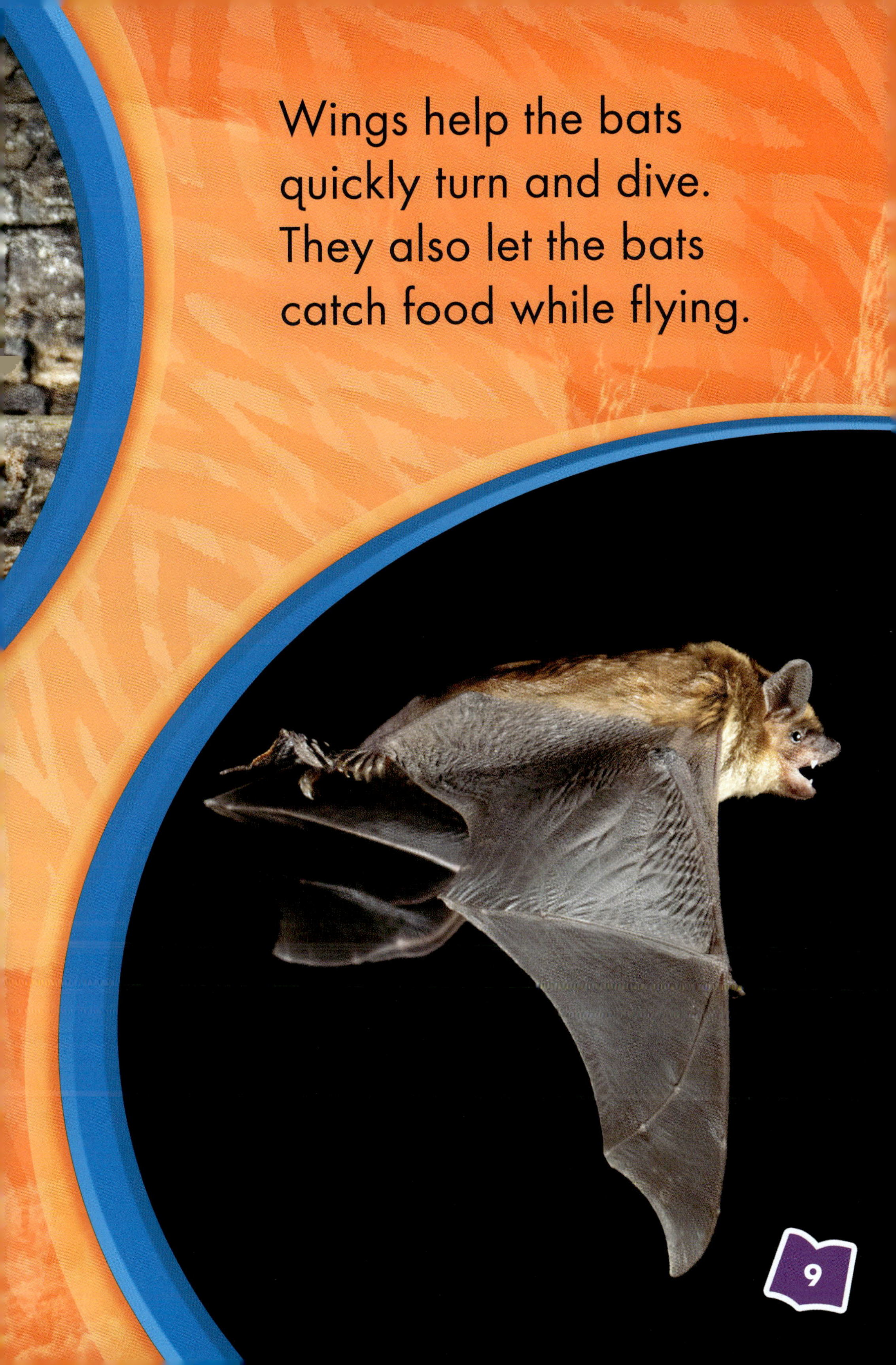

Wings help the bats quickly turn and dive. They also let the bats catch food while flying.

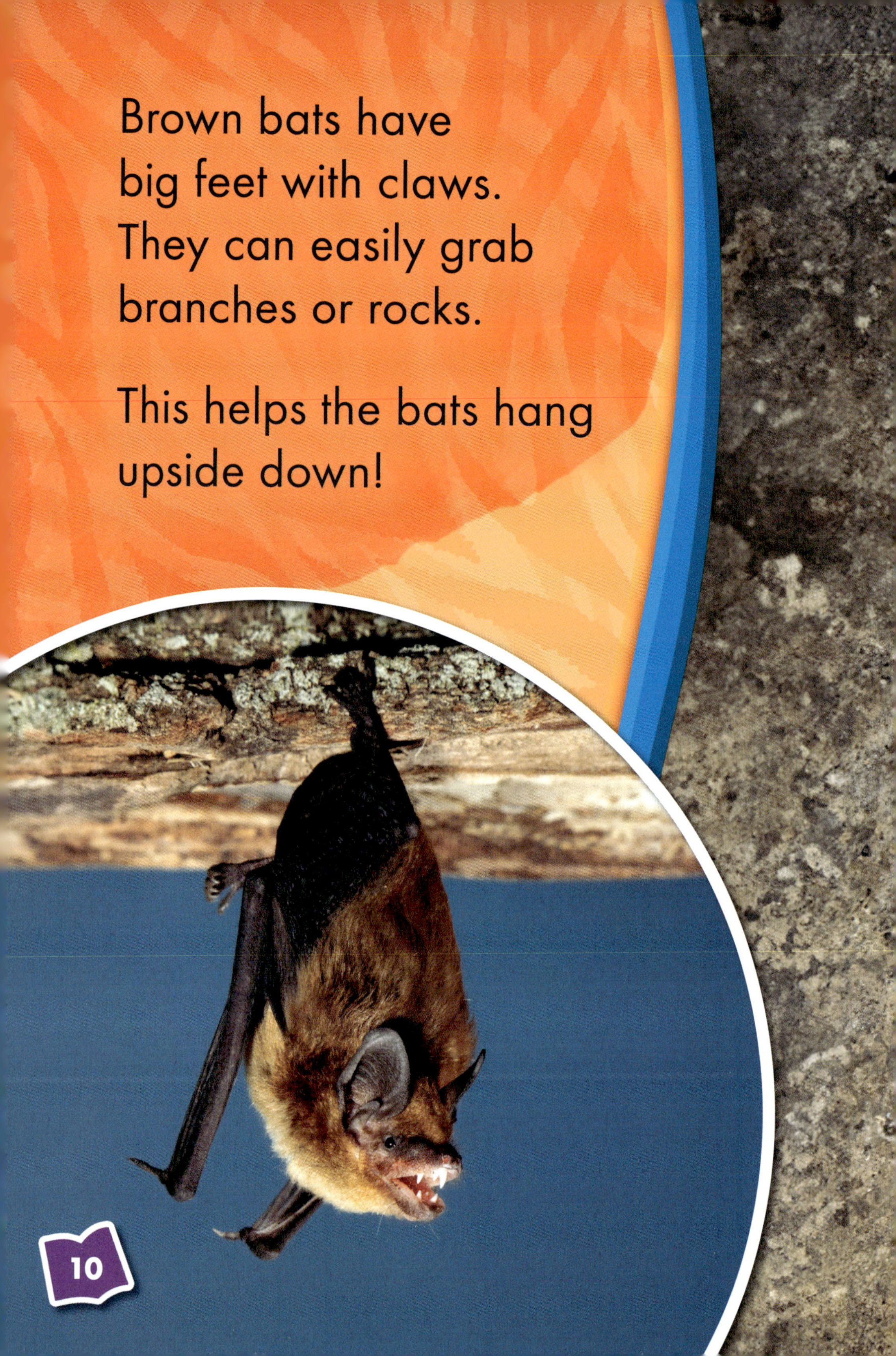

Brown bats have big feet with claws. They can easily grab branches or rocks.

This helps the bats hang upside down!

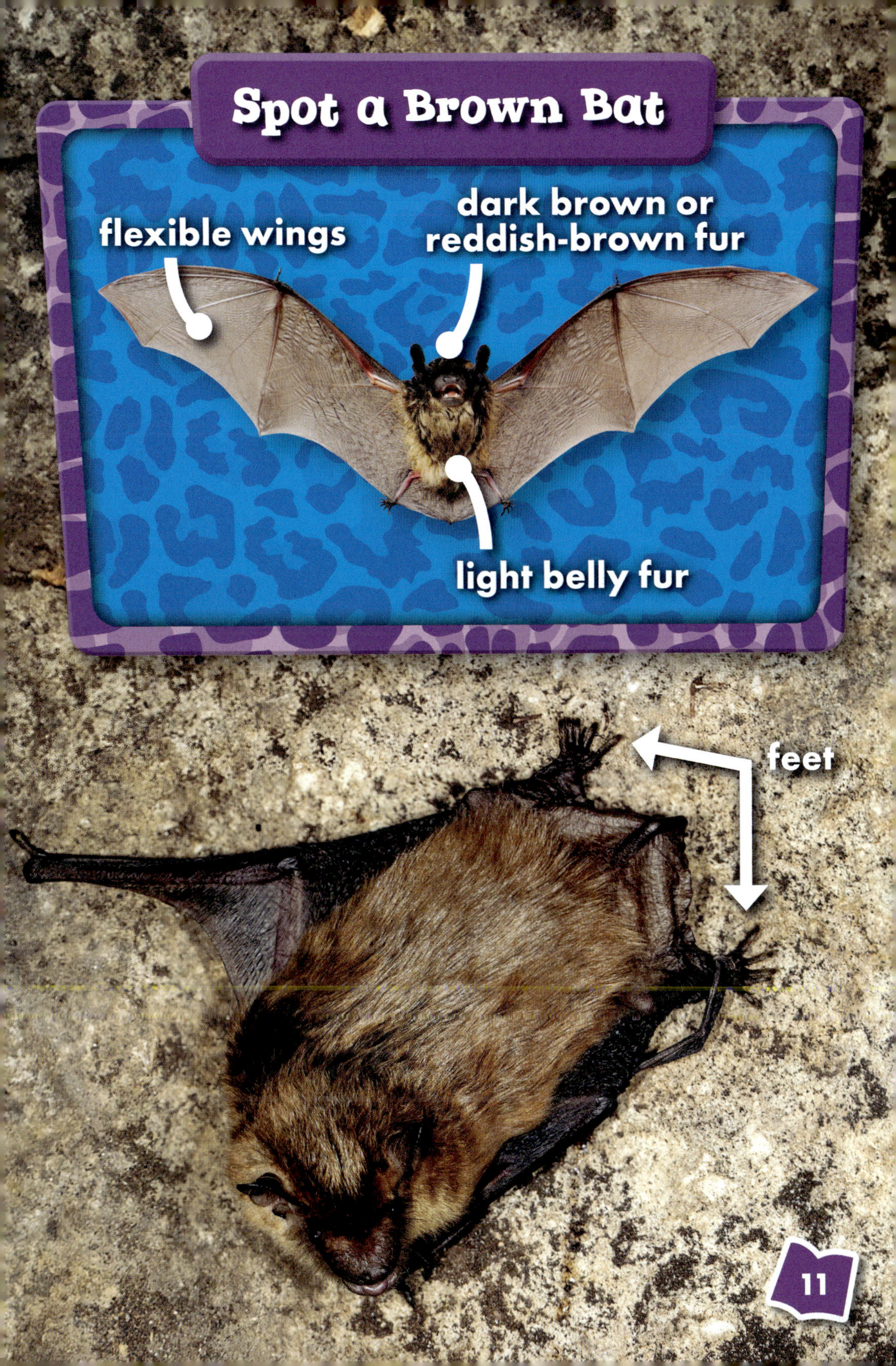
Spot a Brown Bat
flexible wings
dark brown or reddish-brown fur
light belly fur
feet

Pest Control!

cave

Brown bats live in caves, cities, and forests. They **roost** in **colonies**.

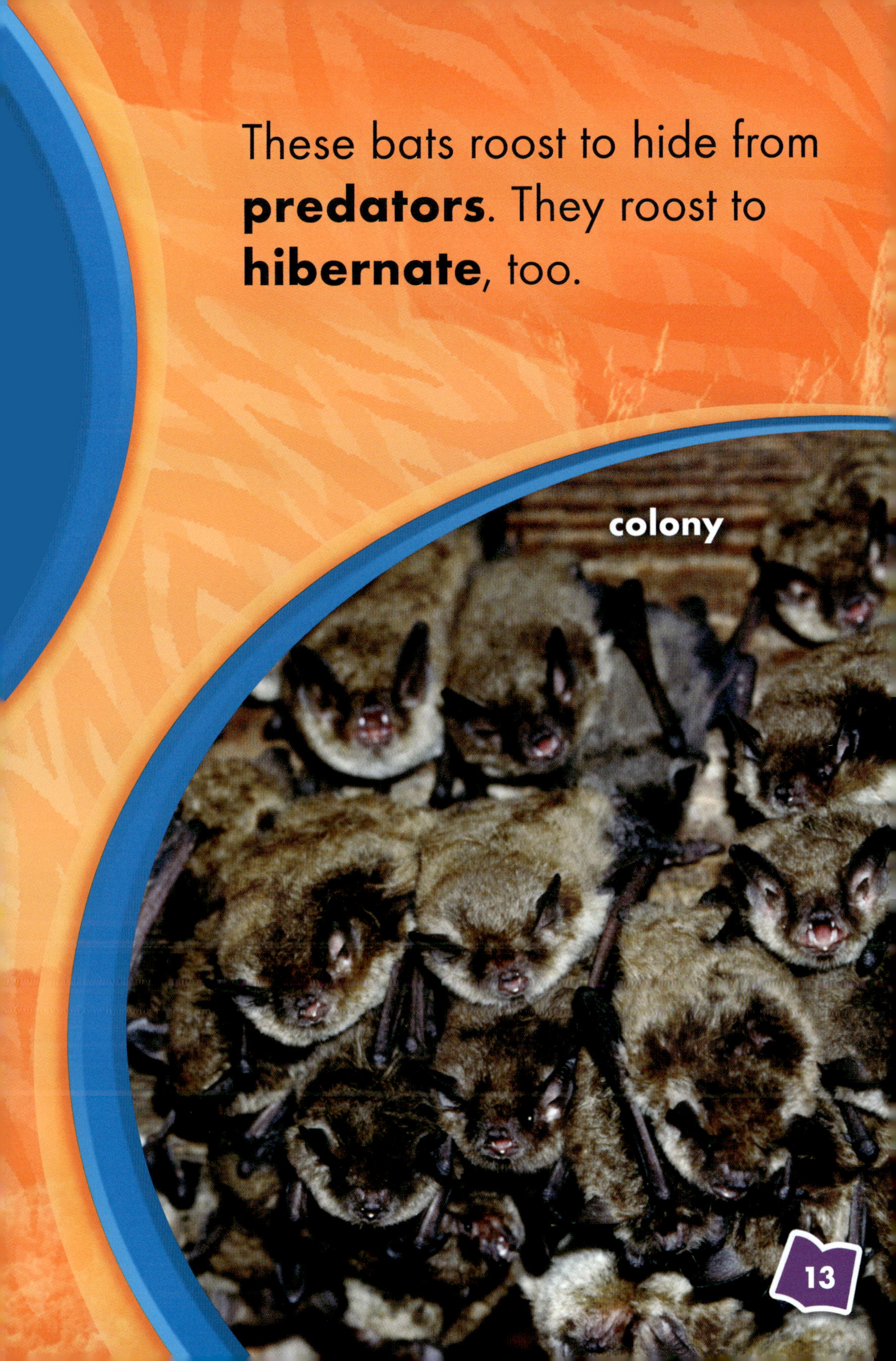

These bats roost to hide from **predators**. They roost to **hibernate**, too.

Brown bats are **nocturnal**.
They hunt at night.

They are **insectivores**. They eat mosquitoes and beetles. They may eat 1,000 insects an hour!

Brown bats use **echolocation** to find insects to eat. Their squeaks **bounce** off insects and back to their ears.

The sounds tell bats where insects are!

Growing Up

Female brown bats give birth to one or two **pups** at once. Pups are born without fur.

Pups need their mothers for food. Mothers also keep their pups warm.

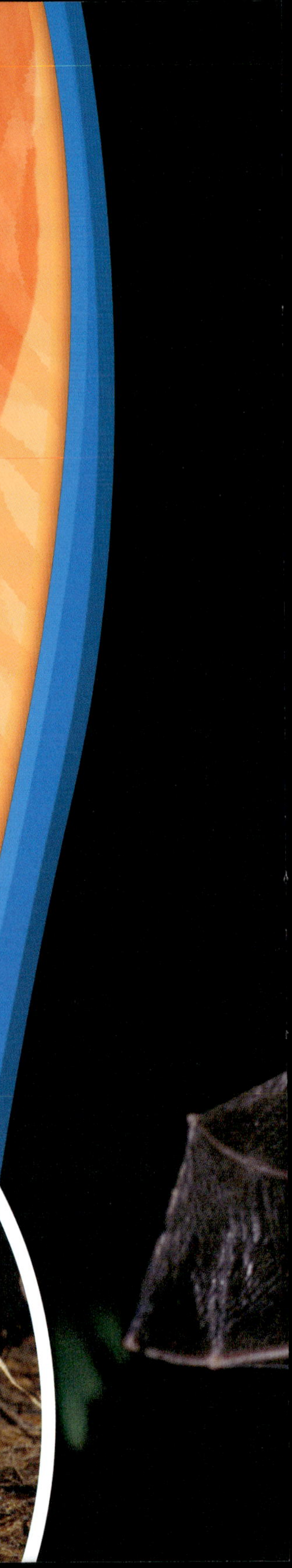

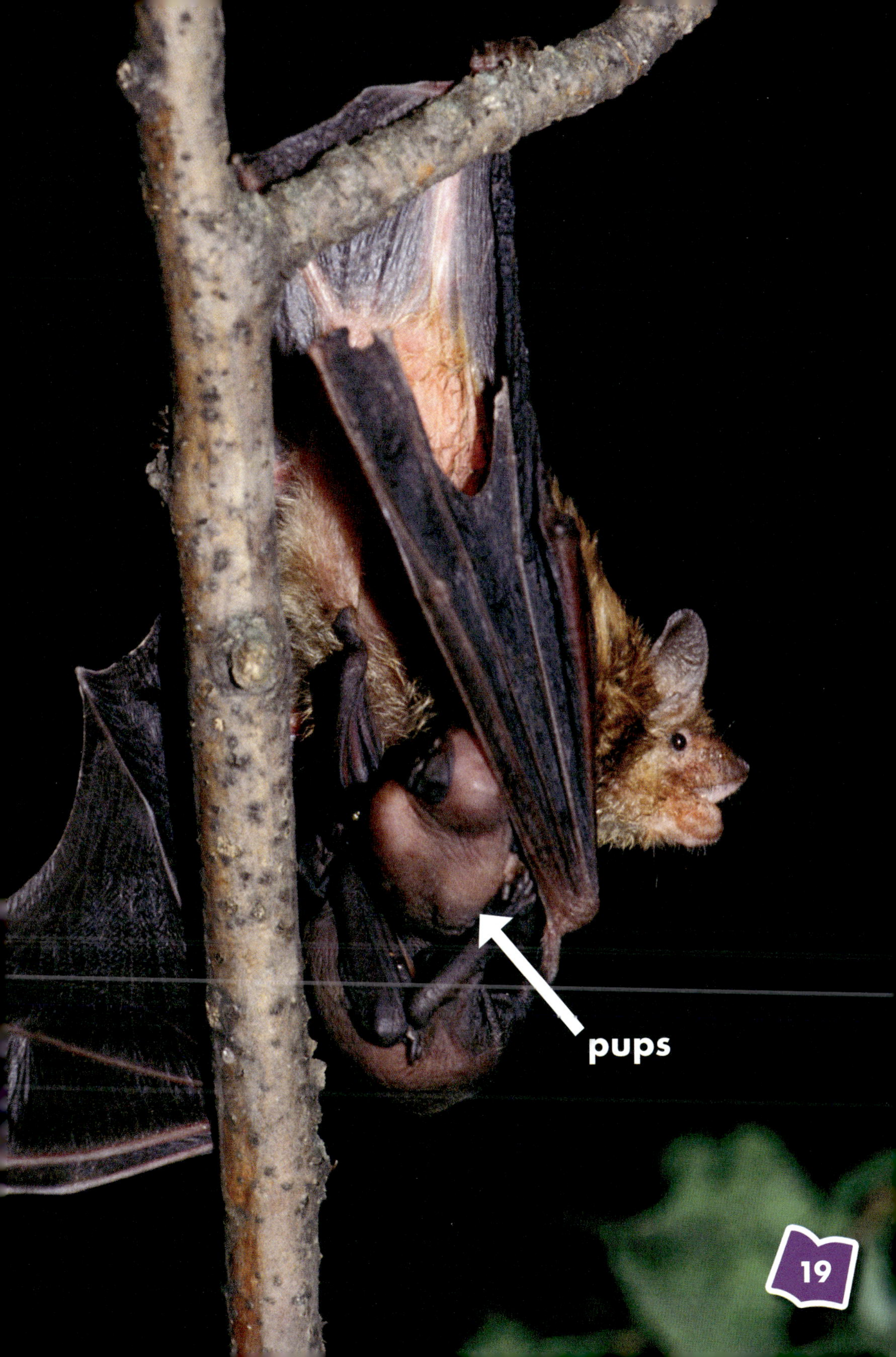
pups

By one month old, pups learn to fly. They also learn to hunt.

Then they leave their mothers. These bats can live for many years!

Glossary

bounce—to come back after hitting something

colonies—groups of brown bats

echolocation—the process of finding objects or animals using sound waves

flexible—able to bend

hibernate—to pass the winter by sleeping or resting

insectivores—animals that only eat insects; insects are small animals with six legs and bodies divided into three parts.

mammals—warm-blooded animals that have backbones and feed their young milk

nocturnal—active at night

predators—animals that hunt other animals for food

pups—baby brown bats

roost—to rest in high places

To Learn More

AT THE LIBRARY

Jenner, Caryn. *All About Bats.* New York, N.Y.: DK, 2023.

Murray, Julie. *Fun Facts About Bats.* Minneapolis, Minn.: Abdo Zoom, 2022.

Perish, Patrick. *Brown Bats.* Minneapolis, Minn.: Bellwether Media, 2021.

ON THE WEB

Factsurfer.com gives you a safe, fun way to find more information.

1. Go to www.factsurfer.com.
2. Enter "brown bats" into the search box and click 🔍.
3. Select your book cover to see a list of related content.

Index

The images in this book are reproduced through the courtesy of: JasonOndreicka, cover (brown bat); Billy McDonald, cover background, interior background; Creative Designer788, cover (brown bat icon); Liz Webber, p. 3; ClassicStock/ Alamy, p. 4; ondreicka, pp. 6, 17; Dennis Donohue, p. 7; Ivan Kuzmin, pp. 8, 9, 10, 15 (brown bat); Stan, pp. 10-11; IgorCheri, pp. 11, 23; Historic Collection/ Alamy, p. 12; Chronicle/ Alamy, p. 13; Rod Gardner, pp. 14-15; pharry, p. 15 (owls); donyanedomam, p. 15 (hawks); Roziline, p. 15 (mosquitoes); Beatriz Moisset/ Wikipedia, p. 15 (beetles); Michelle Gilders/ Alamy, p. 16; Tom Uhlman/ Alamy, p. 18; Gay Bumgarner/ Alamy, pp. 18-19; Nature Picture Library/ Alamy, p. 20; Bob, p. 21.